# MEDITERRANEAN FOR TWO COOKBOOK

Healthy Mediterranean Cooking for Couples,
Roommates, and Partners

Linda Gilmore

# CONTENTS

# INTRODUCTION

Are you striving for a transformative approach to your nutrition that goes beyond fleeting weight loss trends? Are you striving for a way of eating that will make you feel better and become an integral part of your life? The Mediterranean diet offers a refreshing departure from fleeting fads. Its roots run deep in the Mediterranean region, where entire generations have thrived on its nutritional principles, promoting longevity and enduring vitality.

Unlike many trendy diets focused solely on rapid weight loss, the Mediterranean diet incorporates a holistic approach to health. Traditional diets often impose harsh restrictions, resulting in short-term victories, inevitably followed by breakdowns. Whether you're an Epicurean explorer or a dedicated culinary enthusiast, the Mediterranean diet offers a delicious variety of dishes that will appeal to your palate. Switching to the Mediterranean diet allows you to not deny yourself the pleasure of eating out.

My personal journey reflects the changes that a Mediterranean diet can bring. Throughout my childhood, I rarely gave much thought to the impact of nutrition on my well-being, succumbing to numerous culinary indulgences. And then, I was lucky enough to be introduced to the Mediterranean diet by a college roommate rooted in the sun-drenched landscapes of the Mediterranean. Our shared apartment became a paradise of gastronomic exploration and unfamiliar flavors. I discovered the deep connection between food, health, and happiness in Mediterranean cuisine.

The Mediterranean diet became an integral part of my daily life. Subtle adjustments to my diet resulted in tangible changes - I lost excess weight, but more importantly, I experienced a boost in my overall well-being, both physically and mentally.

This cookbook invites us to explore the Mediterranean diet, a journey that celebrates the art of mindful eating and the joy of cooking for two. Each recipe is thoughtfully crafted to bring out the best flavors of the Mediterranean while catering to the needs of the duo.

In these pages, you'll discover the secrets of Mediterranean cuisine, embark on a journey of shared meals, and ignite a passion for a healthy and energetic lifestyle. Join me as the Mediterranean diet is not just an eating regimen but an enriching journey for two that nourishes the body and soul and allows you to enjoy life.

# WELCOME TO THE MEDITERRANEAN CUISINE

The nutritional approach reflects the culinary traditions of the countries along the Mediterranean coast - Eastern Mediterranean, Southern Europe, and North Africa. It is not just a diet but a reflection of how generations of people in these regions have eaten for centuries.

Like the lands from which it originates, the Mediterranean diet includes aromatic herbs, various ingredients, and a vibrant color palette. It is a harmonious and nutritious combination of foods that promises satiety and well-being. It has no rigid rules, instead focusing on the freshness and seasonality of ingredients and enjoying the process of eating. Unlike a strict dietary framework, this approach frees you from the need to carefully track macronutrients. In addition, Mediterranean people lead active lifestyles, emphasizing exercise's indispensable role in this lifestyle. It is an all-encompassing philosophy aimed at health and longevity.

The Mediterranean diet focuses on fresh fruits and vegetables, making it a healthy choice that fits easily into various lifestyles. This lifestyle instills a mindful relationship with food, encouraging us to savor every flavor with awareness. This mindful relationship with food naturally reduces calories, promoting mindful eating and easy weight management.

The Mediterranean diet, which includes many protein sources, including fish, seafood, poultry, and eggs, favors foods rich in heart-healthy omega-3 fatty acids. Yogurt, cheese, olive oil, and juicy avocado oil provide calcium intake and healthy fats. The captivating essence of Mediterranean gastronomy lies in the exquisite combination of herbs and spices that adorn the dishes - garlic, rosemary, pepper, nutmeg, and basil create a symphony of flavor.

In keeping with the recommendations of a conventional heart-healthy diet, one should abstain from sweets such as candy and sodas and highly processed foods such as hot dogs, deli meats, and packaged snacks. Following the Mediterranean diet, you embark on a culinary and lifestyle journey that honors tradition, enriches your well-being, and invites you into the art of enjoying nutritious and flavorful food.

# COOKING FOR TWO: TIPS AND TRICKS

Cooking for two is a delightful and intimate culinary experience that brings you closer to the heart of Mediterranean cuisine. Incorporating the flavors and traditions of this region with the needs of a duo in mind can be a rewarding adventure. Here are some practical tips and guidelines to help you create Mediterranean meals for two:

## Portioning ingredients:

Adapting recipes for two people requires careful consideration of ingredient quantities. Consider proportions when choosing ingredients to ensure the perfect balance of dishes.

## Freshness is key:

The essence of Mediterranean cuisine is using fresh, high-quality ingredients. Choose seasonal produce, herbs, and spices to enhance the flavors of your dishes.

## Versatile products:

Stock on versatile foods such as olive oil, whole grains, legumes, and nuts. These ingredients can be used in various dishes, enhancing their flavor and nutritional value.

## Modular recipes:

Give preference to recipes that can be customized. For example, you can prepare a basic recipe and add different proteins, vegetables, or seasonings according to your preferences.

## Batch cooking and freezing:

Consider batch cooking ingredients, such as grains, sauces, or roasted vegetables. Freeze portions for future meals, and then weekday cooking will become easy.

## Balanced meals:

The Mediterranean diet emphasizes a balance of protein, healthy fats, whole grains, flavorful herbs and seasonings, fruits, and vegetables. Create complete meals that include all these elements.

**Mix and match dishes:**

Experiment with mixing and matching different foods to create unique Mediterranean-style meals. Combine salads, sauces, and main dishes to diversify and make a satisfying menu.

**Seafood Selection:**

Take advantage of the sea's bounty by offering a variety of seafood. Favor sustainably farmed fish and shellfish to infuse dishes with essential omega-3 fatty acids.

**Herbs and spices:**

Take advantage of the Mediterranean love of herbs and spices. Experiment with flavorful additions like basil, oregano, thyme, and rosemary to enhance the flavor of your dishes.

**Reasonable portions:**

To avoid overspending and ensure a balanced diet, practice portion control. Watch your portions to avoid overeating and enjoy your meals.

**Share the experience:**

Cooking for two is not only a meal but also an experience. Share the process of preparing, cooking, and eating with your partner or loved one to create lasting memories.

**Celebrate diversity:**

Mediterranean cuisine is a combination of flavors from different regions. Try dishes from Southern Europe, North Africa, and West Asia to bring variety to your meals.

**Get creative with leftovers:**

Turn leftovers into new creations. Turn last night's main course into a flavorful salad or wrap for a quick and hearty lunch.

**Enjoy the journey:**

Cooking together provides a great opportunity to socialize, experiment, and appreciate the joy of creating together. Embrace the journey and savor every culinary moment.

As you embark on this Mediterranean cooking journey for two, remember that our cookbook is not just a guide but an invitation to explore, experiment, and savor the joy of cooking and eating together. Bon Appetit!

# BREAKFAST

# MEDITERRANEAN BRUSCHETTA

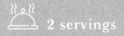 2 servings    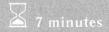 7 minutes     5 minutes

## INGREDIENTS:

- 2 whole-grain bread slices

**For the toppings:**
- ½ mashed avocado/ricotta/ cream cheese/hummus
- 4 green olives, halved
- 2 cherry tomatoes, halved
- 4 oz. (115 g) mozzarella, sliced
- 4 oz. (115 g) sliced Parma ham/ fish/Prosciutto/shredded chicken
- 1 tsp. sunflower/sesame seeds
- to taste

## STEPS:

1. Toast your bread slices using a frying pan/toaster/ air fryer.
2. Arrange all the toppings on the bread toast and sprinkle with seeds.
3. You can customize your toast by adding poached eggs on top.
4. Serve crispy, nutritious toast with morning tea or coffee.

## EACH SERVING HAS:

Calories: 370, Carbs: 26 g, Chol: 40 mg, Sodium: 1301 mg, Fat: 21 g, Protein: 20, Fiber: 8 g, Total Sugars: 5.4 g, Potassium: 704 mg

# OVERNIGHT OATS WITH BERRIES

 2 servings     10 minutes     8 hours

## INGREDIENTS:

- 1 cup (80 g) old-fashioned rolled oats
- 1 cup (240 ml) whole milk/ coconut milk/almond milk/ water
- 1/3 tsp. salt
- 4 Tbsp. fresh raspberries/ strawberries/blueberries
- 2 Tbsp. toasted pine nuts/ cashews/walnuts/pecans
- 2 Tbsp. raspberry jam
- ½ tsp. cinnamon
- 4 Tbsp. peanut butter
- 2 Tbsp. coconut flakes

## STEPS:

1. Mix all the ingredients thoroughly (except the dried bCombine oats, salt, and milk/water in a bowl. Cover and refrigerate overnight.
2. You can serve oats warm or cold.
3. Garnish with peanut butter, coconut flakes, fresh/ frozen berries, or jam. Sprinkle with ground cinnamon.

## EACH SERVING HAS:

Calories: 554, Carbs: 55 g, Chol: 12 mg, Protein: 19.1 g, Fat: 30.1 g, Sodium: 197 mg, Fiber: 7.9 g, Sugar: 19.1 g

# VEGETABLE FRITTATA

 2 servings      10 minutes      15 minutes

## INGREDIENTS:

- 2 whole eggs
- 2 Tbsp. heavy cream/milk
- 4 oz. (100 g) asparagus
- 1 small bell pepper (100 g), sliced
- 1 small red onion, diced
- 2 Roma tomatoes, diced
- ½ cup (60 g) goat cheese, crumbled
- ¼ tsp. dried rosemary/thyme
- salt and black pepper, to taste
- microgreens, for sprinkling
- olive/avocado oil spray

## STEPS:

1. Preheat an oven to 400F (205C).
2. Whisk heavy cream/milk with eggs, dried herbs, salt, and pepper.
3. Spray a baking pan with olive oil.
4. Arrange vegetables and cheese in the baking pan. You can customize your frittata by adding zucchini/spinach/tomatoes/broccoli/mushrooms. Or replace goat cheese with mozzarella/grated Parmesan. Try to slightly fry your vegetables until tender before baking.
5. Pour the milk-egg mixture over the vegetables.
6. Bake for 15–20 minutes.
7. Serve with crispy bread, poultry muffins, or seasonal salad.

## EACH SERVING HAS:

Calories: 240, Total Carbs: 9.9 g, Total Fat: 18 g, Chol: 193 mg, Sodium 122 mg, Protein: 13 g, Fiber: 2.9 g, Sugar: 6.6 g

# CHEESY GARLIC BAGUETTE

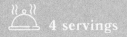 4 servings      10 minutes      15 minutes

## INGREDIENTS:

- 2 Tbsp. unsalted butter, softened
- 2 Tbsp. mayonnaise
- ½ tsp. garlic powder
- ½ tsp. onion powder
- 1 cup (100 g) mozzarella, shredded
- ¼ cup (50 g) olives, chopped

## STEPS:

1. Preheat your oven to 350F (177C).
2. Combine butter, mayonnaise, onion powder, garlic powder, olives, and shredded cheese in a bowl. Stir until smooth and creamy.
3. Spread the mixture over the baguette halves.
4. Arrange the stuffed bread on a baking sheet and bake for 10–12 minutes until the cheese has melted.
5. Transfer to the serving platter and let it cool for 5 minutes. Serve warm with morning tea.

## EACH SERVING HAS:

Calories: 310, Total Fat: 19 g, Saturated Fat: 8.9 g, Chol: 36 mg, Sodium: 480 mg, Carbs: 10.9 g, Dietary Fiber: 1.5 g, Total Sugars: 1.9 g, Protein: 7.7 g, Vitamin D: 0 mcg, Calcium: 43 mg, Iron: 2 mg, Potassium: 76 mg

# APPETIZERS & MEZZE

| | |
|---|---|
| Romesco Sauce | 24 |
| Baba Ganoush | 26 |
| Labneh Dip | 28 |

# ROMESCO SAUCE

# ROMESCO SAUCE

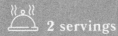 2 servings   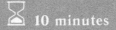 10 minutes

## INGREDIENTS:

- 1 red bell pepper (130 g), roasted and diced
- ½ cup (80 g) toasted almonds/ walnuts/pecans
- ½ cup (80 g) sun-dried tomatoes
- 2 Tbsp. olive oil
- 2 garlic cloves, roasted in a foil for 15 minutes
- 2 Tbsp. lemon juice
- ½ tsp. smoked paprika
- ¼ tsp. cayenne pepper
- ¼ tsp. kosher salt
- ¼ tsp. brown sugar

## STEPS:

1. Add all the ingredients to a food processor/ blender and blend into a smooth paste.
2. Store it in a fridge for 6-8 days.
3. Serve it as a dip with vegetable wedges, crispy bread, pita, or crackers. You can also use Romesco sauce for cooking poultry or meat.

## EACH SERVING HAS:

Calories: 291, Total Fat: 28 g, Chol: 0 mg, Sodium: 4 mg, Carbs: 11 g, Fiber: 3.9 g, Total Sugars: 4 g, Protein: 6.4 g

# BABA GANOUSH

# BABA GANOUSH

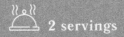 2 servings 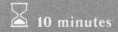 10 minutes  40 minutes

## INGREDIENTS:

- 1 small eggplant (10 oz./300 g)
- 1 Tbsp. sesame oil/olive oil
- 1 Tbsp. tahini
- 1 tsp. lemon juice
- 2 garlic cloves, peeled
- A pinch of salt
- 1/8 tsp. ground nutmeg
- ¼ tsp. paprika/chili

## STEPS:

1. Preheat an oven to 425F (220C).
2. Wrap the garlic cloves in aluminum foil.
3. Poke the eggplant skin with the fork a few times and wrap it in aluminum foil.
4. Bake the garlic in the oven for 15 minutes and the eggplant for 40 minutes. You can grill the eggplant if you like the smoky flavor.
5. Let the eggplant cool, then peel and chop. Let it drain for 5 minutes.
6. Add the baked eggplant, cooked garlic cloves, tahini, lemon juice, salt, olive oil, and nutmeg to the food processor and make a smooth paste.
7. Transfer eggplant puree to a serving bowl and garnish with paprika. Serve with pita bread, crisp veggies (fresh or grilled), or lettuce leaves.
8. Baba Ghanoush is a perfect addition to an appetizing board.

## EACH SERVING HAS:

Calories: 109, Total Carbs: 8.4 g, Total Fat: 7.5 g, Chol: 0 mg, Sodium 12 mg, Protein: 2.3 g, Fiber: 4.8 g, Sugar: 3.6 g

# LABNEH DIP

# LABNEH DIP

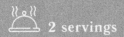 2 servings     15 minutes     12 hours

## INGREDIENTS:

- 1 cup (240 ml) plain Greek yogurt
- A pinch of salt
- ¼ cup olives, chopped
- 1 tsp. extra virgin olive oil
- 1 tsp. fresh parsley, chopped
- ½ tsp. lemon zest
- ¼ tsp. ground sumac

## STEPS:

1. Line a strainer with four layers of cheesecloth. Place it over a deep bowl.
2. Season the yogurt with salt and pour it into the cheesecloth. Refrigerate for 12–24 hours.
3. Discard the liquid collected in the bowl.
4. Transfer the thickened yogurt to a serving bowl and drizzle with olive oil.
5. Garnish with chopped olives, parsley, lemon zest, and sumac before serving.
6. Serve with crunchy vegetables or add to salads, soups, or pizzas. You can also use it as a spread for sandwiches or pita bread.

## EACH SERVING HAS:

Calories: 29, Total Fat: 2.3 g, Chol: 0 mg, Sodium: 45 mg, Carbs: 1.2 g, Fiber: 0.2 g, Total Sugars: 0.7 g, Protein: 2 g

# SALADS & SIDES

| | |
|---|---|
| Vegetable Salad with Lentils | 32 |
| Artichoke Salad | 34 |
| Greek Salad | 36 |
| Roasted Zucchini | 38 |

# VEGETABLE SALAD WITH LENTILS

 2 servings   10 minutes   20 minutes

## INGREDIENTS:

- ½ cup (100 g) lentils, soaked
- 2 cherry tomatoes (40 g), wedges
- 2 garlic cloves, minced
- 2 Tbsp. extra virgin olive oil
- ¼ tsp. cumin
- ¼ tsp. coriander
- ¼ tsp. turmeric
- ½ tsp. mint
- ½ tsp. smoked paprika
- ½ white onion (35 g), chopped
- a handful of spinach
- salt, to taste
- ½ Tbsp. tahini
- ½ lime, juiced
- 1 small cucumber, diced
- 1 Roma tomato, chopped
- ½ white onion (35 g), diced

## STEPS:

1. Add diced cucumber, tomatoes, diced onion, and 1 tablespoon olive oil to a bowl and mix well. Set it aside.

2. Cook your chopped onion, 1 tablespoon of olive oil, and sliced garlic cloves in a pan over medium-high heat for 2 minutes.

3. Add spices, hopped Roma tomato, and lentils. Season with salt and add about ½ cup (120 ml) of water to cover the mixture completely. Cover with a lid and simmer for 10–15 minutes.

4. Add spinach and cook for 5 minutes. Add more water if needed.

5. Mix tahini, lime juice, and a pinch of salt in a small bowl. Add 2–3 tablespoons of water until you reach your desired creaminess.

6. Combine the fresh salad with the cooked lentil mixture.

7. Arrange the bowls and serve. Garnish with fresh lettuce leaves and lemon wedges.

## EACH SERVING HAS:

Calories: 418, Carbs: 53 g, Chol: 0 mg, Sodium: 34 mg, Protein: 18 g, Fat: 17 g, Fiber: 20 g, Sugar: 12 g

# ARTICHOKE SALAD

 2 servings    10 minutes

## INGREDIENTS:

- ¼ tsp. crushed red pepper
- ½ tsp. dried oregano
- ½ tsp. dried basil
- 2 Tbsp. olive oil
- ¼ tsp. garlic powder
- 1 cup (55 g) sun-dried tomatoes, chopped
- 1½ cups (250 g) marinated artichoke hearts, cut into bite-size pieces
- 1 cup fresh arugula
- ½ cup (90 g) olives
- salt and pepper, to taste
- ½ Tbsp. white wine vinegar

## STEPS:

1. Combine all the vegetables in a large bowl.
2. Mix the garlic powder, olive oil, rosemary, thyme, pepper, salt, and vinegar in a small bowl.
3. Drizzle dressing over the vegetables and serve..

## EACH SERVING HAS:

Calories: 356, Total Fat: 32.1 g, Chol: 1 mg, Sodium: 627 mg, Carbs: 10.9 g, Fiber: 2 g, Total Sugars: 22.7 g, Protein: 1 g

# GREEK SALAD

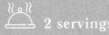 2 servings  10 minutes

## INGREDIENTS:

- 1 red/yellow/green bell pepper (130 g), diced
- 1 tomato/4 cherry tomatoes, diced
- 1 cucumber, diced
- ½ red onion, diced/green onion
- ½ tsp. dried rosemary
- 2 Tbsp. olive oil
- 1 cup baby arugula
- ½ cup black olives/Kalamata olives, pitted
- ½ Tbsp. lemon juice/red wine vinegar
- 1 hard-boiled egg, diced
- ½ cup feta cheese, cubed

## STEPS:

1. Combine all the vegetables in a large bowl. Look for vegetables (except the onion) of a similar size or use only an equal amount.
2. Mix olive oil, dried oregano, and lemon juice in a small bowl. Pour the dressing over the vegetables.
3. Transfer to a serving platter and top with coarsely diced eggs and feta cubes.

## EACH SERVING HAS:

Calories: 265, Total Fat 19.9 g, Chol: 81 mg, Sodium: 338 mg, Total Carbs: 20 g, Fiber: 4.8 g, Total Sugars: 10 g, Protein: 5.9 g

# ROASTED ZUCCHINI

# ROASTED ZUCCHINI

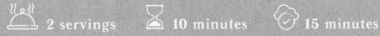 2 servings     10 minutes     15 minutes

## INGREDIENTS:

- 1 medium zucchini, diced
- salt and pepper. to taste
- ¼ tsp. cumin
- 1 Tbsp. olive oil, divided
- 1 Tbsp. lemon juice
- 1 garlic clove, minced
- 2 Tbsp. fresh dill, chopped
- 1 Tbsp. fresh basil, chopped
- ½ cup (60 g) feta cheese, crumbled

## STEPS:

1. Preheat an oven to 425F (220C).
2. Season zucchini with salt, pepper, cumin, and olive oil.
3. Place zucchini rings in a single layer on a baking sheet. Bake for 10–15 minutes, flipping once.
4. Transfer baked zucchini to a serving plate. Sprinkle with crumbled feta cheese, lemon juice, garlic, and chopped herbs.
5. Serve with roasted pork chops, fried potato, or grilled salmon.

## EACH SERVING HAS:

Calories: 150, Total Carbs: 9.1 g, Fat: 9 g, Protein: 5 g, Sodium 235 mg, Fiber: 2 g, Sugar: 2 g

# FISH & SEAFOOD

# CRISPY GARLIC SHRIMP

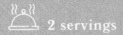 2 servings    5 minutes   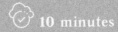 10 minutes

## INGREDIENTS:

- ½ lb. (225 g) raw shrimp, peeled and deveined
- 1 garlic clove, minced
- ¼ tsp. anise seeds
- 1 Tbsp. unsalted butter
- salt and black pepper, to taste
- 1 Tbsp. fresh parsley, finely chopped
- 2 lemon wedges, for sprinkling

## STEPS:

1. Combine shrimp with garlic, anise seeds, salt, and pepper.
2. Melt butter in a frying pan. Add shrimp and cook for 10 minutes until golden, stirring occasionally.
3. Sprinkle with chopped parsley and lemon juice.
4. Serve crispy garlic shrimp in a sauce with pasta, rice, and beans as an ingredient in a salad or cocktail, an appetizer, or a separate dish.

## EACH SERVING HAS:

Calories: 172, Carbs: 3.9 g, Chol: 236 mg, Sodium: 277 mg, Fat: 5.1 g, Protein: 27 g, Fiber: 0.7 g, Total Sugars: 0.4 g, Potassium: 229 mg

# SALMON WITH VEGETABLES

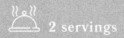 2 servings 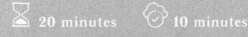 20 minutes  10 minutes

## INGREDIENTS:

- 2 salmon/white fish fillets (6 oz./180 g each)
- olive oil and unsalted butter
- 1 Tbsp. lemon juice, for sprinkling

FOR THE MARINADE

- 1 Tbsp. olive oil
- 2 Tbsp. lemon juice
- 1 garlic clove, crushed
- 1 Tbsp. dried oregano/fresh chopped oregano

FOR THE SALAD

- 2 tomatoes (300 g), chopped
- 1 small bell pepper (100 g), chopped
- 1 small red onion (50 g), diced
- 1 cup lettuce, chopped
- ½ cup feta cheese, cubed
- 1 Tbsp. olive oil
- ½ Tbsp. white wine vinegar
- ½ Tbsp. fresh lemon juice
- ½ tsp. dried rosemary
- Salt, to taste

## STEPS:

1. Mix all the ingredients for the marinade in a bowl and coat the salmon fillets in it. Let the salmon marinate for 20 minutes.

2. Heat olive oil and butter in a frying pan over medium-high heat. Fry marinated salmon fillets for 8 minutes until golden brown, flipping once.

3. Combine all the vegetables for the salad and add feta cheese on top. You can replace the fresh vegetables with roasted or baked ones for a smoky flavor.

4. Mix all the ingredients for the dressing in a small bowl. Pour it over the salad.

5. Transfer the salad on a serving platter and serve with the salmon.

## EACH SERVING HAS:

Calories: 449, Total Carbs: 12.3 g, Total Fat: 29 g, Chol: 103 mg, Sodium 399 mg, Protein: 41 g, Fiber: 3 g, Sugar: 6.9 g

# BAKED WHITE FISH WITH VEGETABLES

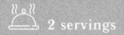 2 servings  10 minutes  15 minutes

## INGREDIENTS:

- 1 lb. (450 g) white fish filet (halibut/cod)
- Salt and pepper, to taste
- 2 Tbsp. olive oil
- 1 lemon, juiced
- 6 cherry tomatoes
- ½ medium zucchini, chopped
- 1 small carrot (45 g), chopped
- 2 tbsp. red onion, diced
- 3 garlic cloves, minced
- 1 Tbsp. fresh parsley
- 2 tsp. dried basil

## STEPS:

1. CPreheat the oven to 425F (220C). Grease a baking dish with olive oil.
2. Pat white fish dry and season with salt and pepper.
3. Arrange the fish on the baking dish and sprinkle with lemon juice.
4. Coat the fish with vegetables and season with salt and pepper.
5. Bake for 15–20 minutes, stirring halfway through.
6. Serve sprinkled with fresh lemon juice and chopped parsley.

## EACH SERVING HAS:

Calories: 460, Carbs: 23 g, Chol: 69 mg, Sodium: 155 mg, Protein: 49 g, Fat: 20 g, Fiber: 6 g, Total Sugars: 15 g

# SEAFOOD PAELLA

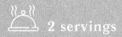 2 servings    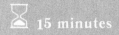 15 minutes     50 minutes

## INGREDIENTS:

- ½ cup (100 g) short-grain rice (Bomba, Calasparra, Arborio)
- 1 cup (240 ml) chicken stock, hot
- 1 pinch of saffron thread
- 5 oz. (150 g) shrimp/prawns, peeled and deveined
- 5 oz. (150 g) mussels, scrubbed and debearded
- ½ red onion (35 g), chopped
- 2 garlic cloves, minced
- 1 tomato (80 g), chopped
- 2 Tbsp. frozen peas, thawed
- 2 Tbsp. olive oil
- ½ tsp. smoked paprika
- ¼ tsp. red pepper flakes
- 3 oz. (80 g) green beans
- ½ cup fresh parsley, chopped
- salt, to taste

## STEPS:

1. Heat olive oil in a deep pan over medium heat.
2. Add chopped onion and cook for 2 minutes until tender. Add rice and cook for 3 minutes, stirring often. You can use any grain you choose, but rice is perfect because it has a neutral taste and absorbs spicy, rich flavors from the add-ins.
3. Add minced garlic, chopped tomatoes, green beans, peas, saffron thread, paprika, and red pepper flakes and cook for 1 minute, stirring often.
4. Add 2 cups of chicken stock and bring to a boil. Cook for 5–10 minutes, stirring occasionally.
5. Reduce the heat to low, cover with a lid, and simmer for 20 minutes.
6. Open the lid, stir in shrimp and mussels, close the lid, and cook for 10 minutes. Add stock or water if needed.
7. You can customize the recipe by adding chorizo, various seafood, white fish (cod, halibut), or meat chunks.
8. Serve warm with lemon wedges.

## EACH SERVING HAS:

Calories 843, Total Fat 10.7 g, Saturated Fat 2 g, Chol: 171 mg, Sodium 701 mg, Total Carbs: 143 g, Dietary Fiber 5.3 g, Total Sugars 3.4 g, Protein 35 g, Calcium 162 mg, Iron 9 mg, Potassium 679 mg

# GARLIC SCALLOPS

 2 servings   7 minutes   5 minutes

## INGREDIENTS:

- ½ lb. (225 g) dry sea scallops
- 1 garlic clove, minced
- ½ Tbsp. lemon juice
- 1 Tbsp. fresh rosemary, chopped
- 1 Tbsp. ghee/butter, melted
- ¼ tsp. smoked paprika
- 1 Tbsp. olive oil
- salt and pepper, to taste
- lemon slices and watercress, for garnish

## STEPS:

1. Season scallops with salt and pepper.
2. Melt butter in a skillet over medium heat. Add minced garlic.
3. Place scallops in a single layer in the skillet. Fry for 5 minutes until golden, flipping once. Take care not to overcook them.
4. Combine lemon juice, paprika, chopped basil, olive oil, salt, and pepper in a bowl.
5. Transfer scallops to a serving platter and sprinkle with the lemon dressing. Garnish with watercress and lemon slices.
6. Serve with roasted asparagus, Brussels sprouts, cauliflower, or your favorite dipping sauce.

## EACH SERVING HAS:

Calories: 119, Total Fat: 2.5 g, Chol: 35 mg, Sodium: 185 mg, Total Carbs: 5.4 g, Fiber: 1.4 g, Total Sugars: 0.4 g, Protein: 22 g

# POULTRY

# LEMON CHICKEN THIGHS

 2 servings  10 minutes
(plus 1 hour for marinating)
 60 minutes

## INGREDIENTS:

- 2 chicken thighs, bone-in and skin-on
- 2 Tbsp. lemon juice
- 2 lemon slices
- 1 tsp. dried oregano
- ¼ tsp. paprika
- ½ tsp. onion powder
- 2 garlic cloves, crushed
- salt and pepper, to taste
- 1 Tbsp. olive oil

## STEPS:

1. Combine olive oil, lemon juice, oregano, onion powder, paprika, salt, and pepper. Coat the chicken thighs and marinate them for 60 minutes.
2. Preheat an oven to 400F (205C).
3. Place chicken thighs on a baking dish. Sprinkle the remaining marinade over the chicken. Top with lemon slices and rosemary sprigs.
4. Bake for 50–60 minutes until golden.
5. Serve with rice, fresh salad, and marinara sauce.

## EACH SERVING HAS:

Calories: 301, Total Carbs: 3.9 g, Total Fat: 23.5 g, Cholesterol 88 mg, Sodium 173 mg, Protein: 18.5 g, Fiber: 1 g, Sugar: 2 g

# GREEK TURKEY CUTLETS

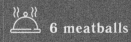 6 meatballs      10 minutes     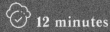 12 minutes

## INGREDIENTS:

- ½ lb. (225 g) ground turkey/ chicken
- ½ cup (30 g) fresh spinach, chopped/broccoli/fresh greens
- 2 oz. (50 g) feta/mozzarella, shredded
- ½ cup bell pepper (50 g), finely chopped
- ½ yellow onion (35 g), finely chopped
- 1 garlic clove, minced
- 1 whole egg, slightly beaten
- 2 Tbsp. breadcrumbs
- Salt, to taste
- 2 Tbsp. olive oil, for frying

## STEPS:

1. Mix all the ingredients in a bowl. Form small patties from the mixture using your hands.
2. Preheat olive oil in the skillet.
3. Fry patties for 8–12 minutes until golden brown, flipping them once.
4. Serve warm with seasonal salad, mashed potato, and sauce of your choice.

## EACH SERVING HAS:

Calories: 161, Total Carbs: 3.6 g, Total Fat: 10.9 g, Chol: 61 mg, Sodium 171 mg, Protein: 12.5 g, Fiber: 0.9 g, Sugar: 1.4 g

# STUFFED CHICKEN BREAST

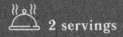 2 servings 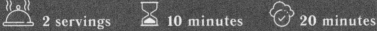 10 minutes 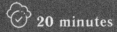 20 minutes

## INGREDIENTS:

- 2 chicken breasts
- 4 oz. (110 g) mozzarella/feta cheese, shredded
- 4 sun-dried tomatoes, chopped
- 8 black olives, diced
- 1 Tbsp. thyme
- salt, black pepper, paprika
- olive oil

## STEPS:

1. Carefully cut the chicken breasts horizontally, making a pocket.
2. Mix shredded feta cheese, chopped sun-dried tomatoes, chopped olives, thyme, salt, and pepper.
3. Stuff the chicken pockets with cheese mixture. Brush the outside of the chicken breasts with olive oil and season with salt, paprika, and pepper.
4. Heat olive oil in a frying pan over medium heat.
5. Fry the stuffed chicken breasts on each side until brown.
6. Serve with grilled asparagus or broccoli.

## EACH SERVING HAS:

Calories: 579, Total Carbs: 13.1 g, Total Fat: 33 g, Chol: 169 mg, Sodium 415 mg, Protein: 60 g, Fiber: 4.4 g, Sugar: 6.7 g

# CHICKEN SOUVLAKI

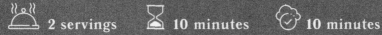 2 servings     10 minutes     10 minutes

## INGREDIENTS:

- 1 lb. (450 g) chicken/pork/ beef/lamb fillets, cut into 2" cubes
- 1 Tbsp. dried thyme
- 1 Tbsp. olive oil
- 2 garlic cloves, minced
- ½ tsp. salt
- ½ tsp. red pepper flakes
- ¼ tsp. ground black pepper
- ½ lemon juice

## STEPS:

1. Combine olive oil, lemon juice, herbs, spices, salt, and minced garlic.
2. Coat chicken pieces in the spicy mixture and marinate for 1-2 hours.
3. Thread the marinated meat onto skewers.
4. Preheat your grill.
5. Grill the chicken until golden brown, flipping the skewers occasionally.
6. Serve souvlaki with grilled pita bread, fresh salad, and tomato sauce.

## EACH SERVING HAS:

Calories: 250, Total Carbs: 0.9 g, Total Fat: 13 g, Chol: 99 mg, Sodium 96 mg, Protein: 32.3 g, Fiber: 0.4 g, Sugar: 0.2 g

# VEGETARIAN

**VEGETABLES**

# FRENCH RATATOUILLE

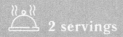 2 servings    10 minutes    25 minutes

## INGREDIENTS:

- 1 tsp. balsamic vinegar
- 1 small bell pepper (100 g), chopped
- ½ eggplant (150 g), chopped
- 2 garlic cloves, minced
- ¼ tsp. ground ginger
- 1 tsp. olive oil
- 2 Tbsp. scallions, finely chopped
- ¼ tsp. dried thyme
- 1 tsp. smoked paprika
- 2 Tbsp. (30 ml) red wine
- salt and pepper, to taste
- fresh parsley, for garnish
- 2 ripe tomatoes, chopped
- 1 tsp. tomato paste
- ½ zucchini (150 g), chopped

## STEPS:

1. Heat olive oil in a frying pan over medium heat and sauté the scallions for 4–5 minutes until golden brown.
2. Add chopped eggplant and garlic to the pan and simmer for 3–4 minutes. Reduce heat to medium-low.
3. Add ground ginger, dried thyme, paprika, salt, and red wine to the pan and simmer for 5–6 minutes, stirring occasionally.
4. Add chopped bell peppers, tomatoes, and zucchini, and cook until tender.
5. Add tomato paste and vinegar and cook for 5–7 minutes.
6. Let it rest for 10 minutes before serving.
7. Sprinkle with chopped parsley and serve with crispy Italian bread.

## EACH SERVING HAS:

Calories: 119, Total Carbs: 18 g, Total Fat 4.5 g, Chol: 0 mg, Sodium 19 mg, Dietary Fiber: 7.4 g, Total Sugars: 9.3 g

# VEGETABLE CASSEROLE

 2 servings  15 minutes 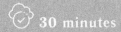 30 minutes

## INGREDIENTS:

- 1 small bell pepper (100 g), chopped
- ½ zucchini (100 g), diced
- 2 green onions, chopped
- ½ cup broccoli florets
- ½ red onion (30 g), diced
- Salt and black pepper, to taste
- 2 Tbsp. extra virgin olive oil
- 3 medium eggs
- ¼ tsp. baking powder (optional)
- 2 Tbsp. (30 ml) whole milk
- ¼ cup (30 g) crumbled feta cheese, plus more for serving
- 2 Tbsp. chopped parsley, plus more for serving
- ½ tsp. fresh oregano

## STEPS:

1. Preheat an oven to 450F (230C).
2. Combine bell peppers, red onion, zucchini, green onion, broccoli, 2 tablespoons of olive oil, and a pinch of salt and black pepper in a bowl.
3. Add the vegetables to the baking pan. Bake them for 15 min. Remove the veggies from the oven.
4. Lower the heat to 400F (205C).
5. Meanwhile, whisk eggs, baking powder (if using), milk, crumbled feta, parsley, oregano, salt, and pepper in a bowl.
6. Arrange baked vegetables in a casserole dish and cover with egg mixture. Bake for 8–10 minutes until set.
7. Sprinkle with crumbled feta and fresh parsley. Serve with crispy French bread.

## EACH SERVING HAS:

Calories: 317, Carbs: 13 g, Protein: 12.9 g, Chol: 260 mg, Sodium: 286 mg, Fat: 24 g, Fiber: 3.2 g, Sugars: 7.7 g

# BAKED VEGETABLES WITH GNOCCHI

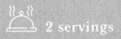 2 servings 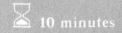 10 minutes 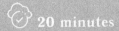 20 minutes

## INGREDIENTS:

- ½ bag (8 oz./225 g) frozen gnocchi or cauliflower gnocchi
- 2 cups (250 g) bell peppers, diced
- ½ zucchini (140 g), cubed
- ½ summer squash (100 g), cubed
- 4 cherry tomatoes, halved
- ½ red onion (40 g), diced
- 2 Tbsp. lemon juice
- 1 Tbsp. avocado oil
- ½ tsp. salt
- ½ tsp. black pepper

## STEPS:

1. Preheat an oven to 425F (218C). Line a baking pan with foil.
2. Mix all the ingredients, except the gnocchi, in a bowl.
3. Spread the mixture on the baking pan. Add gnocchi on top.
4. Bake for 20–25 minutes, stirring twice.
5. Garnish with chopped fresh parsley and serve.

## EACH SERVING HAS:

Calories: 276, Carbs: 56 g, Chol: 13 mg, Sodium: 386 mg, Protein: 10 g, Fat: 3 g, Fiber: 9 g, Sugars: 19 g

# STUFFED BELL PEPPERS

 2 servings 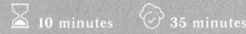 10 minutes 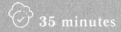 35 minutes

## INGREDIENTS:

- 2 medium bell peppers (150 g each), wide and short
- ½ lb. (225 g) ground beef/ chicken
- ½ cup (100 g) rice, cooked
- 7 oz. (200 g) canned peeled tomatoes, crushed
- ½ yellow onion (30 g), chopped
- 1 garlic clove, minced
- 1 Tbsp. fresh oregano, chopped
- 1 tsp. dried oregano
- ¼ tsp. ground nutmeg
- ¼ tsp. allspice
- ¼ tsp. paprika
- ½ Tbsp. extra-virgin olive oil
- ½ cup (60 g) Mozzarella cheese, grated
- Salt, to taste

## STEPS:

**For the filling:**

1. Heat olive oil in a frying pan over medium heat. Add chopped onion and garlic and simmer for 2–3 minutes until tender.

2. Add ground meat and cook for 5–7 minutes, stirring occasionally.

3. Add rice, seasonings, half of grated cheese, crushed tomatoes, and salt to the pan. Cook for 5 minutes, stirring occasionally.

**For the peppers:**

4. Preheat an oven to 375F (190C).

5. Cut the tops off the peppers and remove everything from the inside. Stuff the peppers with the meat mixture and cover with the tops.

6. You can substitute bell peppers with other vegetables suitable for stuffing, such as zucchini, eggplant, or cabbage leaves.

7. Arrange stuffed peppers on a baking pan. Bake for 15 minutes. Take the peppers out of the oven and remove the tops. Sprinkle the remaining grated cheese over the peppers. Return to the oven and cook for 7–10 minutes.

8. Serve warm, garnished with fresh basil.

## EACH SERVING HAS:

Calories: 329, Total Carbs: 15 g, Sodium 157 mg, Fat: 13 g, Protein: 39 g, Fiber: 4.2 g, Sugar: 11 g

# MEAT

# SAUSAGES WITH VEGETABLES

# SAUSAGES WITH VEGETABLES

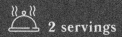 2 servings  10 minutes 15 minutes

## INGREDIENTS:

- 6 oz. (170 g) pre-cooked sausage (Italian/Cajun/Andouille), diced
- ½ bell pepper (80 g), diced
- ½ white onion (40 g), diced
- ½ zucchini, diced
- 1 cup (150 g) corn kernels (optional)
- ½ cup (120 ml) chicken broth
- 1 Tbsp. olive oil
- ¼ tsp. smoked paprika
- 1 Tbsp. spring onion, chopped

## STEPS:

1. Heat olive oil in a frying pan over medium heat.
2. Add diced sausages and cook for 6 minutes until golden brown, flipping once.
3. Remove the sausages from the pan and set aside.
4. Add diced vegetables to the pan and cook for 5 minutes, stirring occasionally.
5. Return sausages to the pan and stir in. Add smoked paprika and chicken broth, and cook for 5 minutes, stirring once.
6. Sprinkle with chopped spring onion and serve with pasta, rice, or crispy Italian bread.

## EACH SERVING HAS:

Calories 467, Total Fat 30 g, Saturated Fat 8.6 g, Chol: 75 mg, Sodium 683 mg, Total Carbs: 30 g, Dietary Fiber 5.3 g, Total Sugars 7.4 g, Protein 22.1 g, Calcium 32 mg, Iron 5 mg, Potassium 850 mg

# LAMB SHANKS WITH TOMATO SAUCE

 2 servings 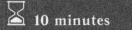 10 minutes  3 hours

## INGREDIENTS:

- 2 lamb shanks
- Salt and pepper, to taste
- 1 Tbsp. olive oil
- 1 onion (70 g), chopped
- 1 carrot (70 g), chopped
- 1 parsnip, chopped
- 1 (14-oz./400 g) can whole Italian plum tomatoes
- ½ cup (120 ml) chicken broth or stock
- ½ cup (120 ml) beef broth or stock
- ½ can chickpeas, drained and rinsed
- 1 teaspoon dried thyme
- Parsley, for garnish

## STEPS:

1. Season lamb shanks with salt and pepper.
2. Heat olive oil in a Dutch oven over medium-high heat. Fry the shanks for 2 minutes per side. Set them aside.
3. Add onions, carrots, and parsnips to the pot, and sauté for 5 to 7 minutes.
4. Add tomatoes, chicken broth, beef broth, chickpeas, and thyme. Bring to a boil.
5. Return the shanks to the pot. Cover the lid and simmer for about 2½ hours or until the meat is tender.
6. Open the lid and cook for 10 minutes or until the juices thicken.
7. Garnish with fresh parsley and serve with crispy bread or country-style potato.

## EACH SERVING HAS:

Calories 458, Total Fat 16 g, Saturated Fat 5 g, Cholesterol 103 mg, Sodium 510 mg, Total Carbohydrate 35 g, Dietary Fiber 10 g, Total Sugars 12.6 g, Protein 42.6 g, Calcium 109 mg, Iron 7 mg, Potassium 1229 mg

# CREAMY PORK ROAST

# CREAMY PORK ROAST

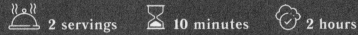 2 servings   10 minutes   2 hours

## INGREDIENTS:

- ½ lb. (225 g) pork, cut into chunks
- 1 Tbsp. olive oil
- 2 oz. (50 g) bacon (or brisket), sliced
- ½ white onion (40 g), chopped
- 2 garlic cloves, minced
- 1 celery raw, stems
- 3 Tbsp. white wine
- 3 Tbsp. water
- ¼ cup (60 ml) heavy cream
- 1 tsp. cornstarch
- 1 tsp. dried thyme
- 10 oz. (300 g) boiled potatoes, for garnish

## STEPS:

1. Preheat the oven to 340F (170C).
2. Heat olive oil in a brazier/Dutch oven and cook pork chunks until golden brown.
3. Fry the sliced bacon/brisket in another pan to a crisp crust. Remove them from the pan.
4. Add chopped onions, garlic, and celery and cook for 3-4 minutes until soft.
5. Add bacon and vegetables to the brazier. Stir in heavy cream, starch, wine, water, thyme, salt, and pepper.
6. Cover the lid and bake for 1 hour.
7. Serve with boiled potato, rice, or pasta.

## EACH SERVING HAS:

Calories 319, Total Fat: 15 g, Saturated Fat: 5 g, Chol: 40 mg, Sodium: 619 mg, Carbs: 31 g, Dietary Fiber: 4.3 g, Total Sugars: 3.6 g, Protein: 12.5 g, Vitamin D: 2 mcg, Calcium: 40 mg, Iron: 1 mg, Potassium: 855 mg

# KOFTA KEBABS

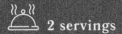 2 servings    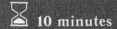 10 minutes     12 minutes

## INGREDIENTS:

- ½ lb. (225 g) ground beef/ lamb
- 1 garlic clove, minced
- 1 small red onion (50 g), finely chopped
- ¼ tsp. nutmeg
- ¼ tsp. allspice
- ¼ tsp. paprika
- 1/8 tsp. ground black pepper
- ¼ tsp. cumin
- ¼ tsp. cardamom
- ¼ tsp. sea salt

## STEPS:

1. Mix all the ingredients in a food processor.
2. Shape 4 oval koftas using your hand. If you prefer, you can string the meat on skewers.
3. Arrange the koftas on a grill or in an air fryer basket in a single layer. Cook at 350F (178C) for 12 minutes until golden brown, flipping once.
4. Serve kofta kebabs with pita bread and grilled vegetables. They perfectly pair with tahini sauce/ baba ganoush/tzatziki sauce/hummus.

## EACH SERVING HAS:

Calories: 161, Carbs: 4 g, Chol: 66 mg, Sodium: 49 mg, Fat: 4.6 g, Protein: 23.1 g, Fiber: 1 g, Total Sugars: 1.2 g, Potassium: 353 mg

# PORK CHOPS IN WINE SAUCE

 2 servings    7 minutes    15 minutes

## INGREDIENTS:

- 2 pork chops (¾-inch (2 cm) thick), bone-in (at room temperature)
- 2 garlic cloves, crushed
- 1 garlic clove, diced
- 8 oz. (225 g) button mushrooms, diced
- ½ cup (120 ml) dry red wine
- ½ cup (120 ml) water
- 10 sprigs of thyme/rosemary
- 2 Tbsp. unsalted butter
- 1 Tbsp. olive oil
- Salt and pepper, to taste

## STEPS:

1. Pat the pork chops dry and rub with crushed garlic, salt, and pepper.
2. Heat olive oil in a frying pan over medium heat. Add garlic and thyme sprigs and cook for 1–2 minutes, stirring occasionally.
3. Add 1 tablespoon of butter and diced mushrooms. Cook for 4–5 minutes until golden.
4. Remove mushrooms, thyme, and garlic from the pan and set aside.
5. Melt the remaining butter in the pan and add pork chops. Cook for 2 minutes on each side until golden.
6. Return mushrooms and garlic to the pan. Add red wine and water. Simmer for 5 minutes, flipping the chops once.
7. Remove from the heat, cover with a lid, and let stand for 5–7 minutes.
8. Serve with roasted potatoes and vegetables. Pour the pork chops with the wine-mushroom sauce from the pan.

## EACH SERVING HAS:

Calories 499, Total Fat 39 g, Saturated Fat 16 g, Chol: 98 mg, Sodium 151 mg, Total Carbs: 7.7 g, Dietary Fiber 1.9 g, Total Sugars 2.4 g, Protein 21 g, Calcium 55 mg, Iron 5 mg, Potassium 739 mg

# GRILLED LAMB CHOPS

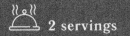 2 servings   10 minutes  15 minutes

## INGREDIENTS:

- 4 lamb chops (1 lb./450 g), patted dry
- garlic salted butter

**For the Marinade:**
- 1 Tbsp. olive oil
- 1 Tbsp. Greek yogurt
- 1 garlic clove, minced
- 1 tsp. fresh rosemary
- ¼ tsp. black pepper
- 1 tsp. lemon juice
- ¼ tsp. lemon zest
- ¼ tsp. sea salt

## STEPS:

1. Mix all the ingredients for the marinade in a bowl.
2. Cover lamb chops with the marinade and let them stand for 2 hours.
3. Preheat your grill or frying pan. Cook for 7–9 minutes for medium-rare and 11–13 minutes for medium-well. Flip halfway through. Drizzle with the remaining marinade every 3–4 minutes.
4. Garnish with fresh rosemary sprigs and thyme.
5. Serve with fresh seasonal salad and arugula leaves.

## EACH SERVING HAS:

Calories: 409, Total Carbs: 0.7 g, Total Fat: 22.2 g, Chol: 175 mg, Sodium 178 mg, Protein: 50 g, Fiber: 0.2 g, Sugar: 0.3 g

# PASTA & GRAINS

| | |
|---|---|
| Mushroom Risotto with Peas | 88 |
| Chicken Casserole | 90 |
| Pasta with Cashew Sauce | 92 |

# MUSHROOM RISOTTO WITH PEAS

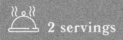 2 servings 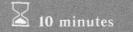 10 minutes 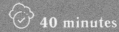 40 minutes

## INGREDIENTS:

- ¾ oz. (20 g) dried porcini mushrooms
- ¾ oz. (20 g) dried shiitake mushrooms
- 4 cups (1 L) low-salt chicken broth
- 2 Tbsp. coconut oil
- 1 small white onion (50 g), finely diced
- ¼ tsp. salt
- ¼ tsp. ground black pepper
- ¾ cup (140 g) Arborio rice
- ¼ cup (60 ml) dry white wine
- 1 cup (120 g) frozen petite peas, thawed
- 1 tsp. balsamic vinegar
- 2 Tbsp. fresh basil, chopped

## STEPS:

1. Place the porcini and the shiitake mushrooms in a large bowl. Add 2 cups of boiling water. Let the mushrooms soak for about 20 minutes. Pat the mushrooms dry with a paper towel.
2. Transfer the mushrooms to a cutting board; discard any stems, then set them aside.
3. Heat oil in a cooking pot. Add chopped onion, salt, and black pepper. Sauté for about 2 minutes.
4. Add rice, mushrooms, and dry wine and cook for 2 minutes, stirring occasionally.
5. Pour in chicken broth and close the lid. Simmer for 20 minutes on medium-high heat.
6. Add peas, vinegar, and basil. Cook for 2 minutes, stirring often.
7. Serve warm, sprinkled with fresh greens.

## EACH SERVING HAS:

Calories 479, Total Fat 12.2 g, Saturated Fat 8.6 g, Chol: 0 mg, Sodium 1599 mg, Total Carbs: 110 g, Dietary Fiber 7.5 g, Total Sugars 5.2 g, Protein 20 g, Calcium 87 mg, Iron 7 mg, Potassium 575 mg

# CHICKEN CASSEROLE

# CHICKEN CASSEROLE

 2 servings    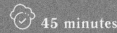 10 minutes    45 minutes

## INGREDIENTS:

- 4 oz. (100 g) penne pasta, cooked
- 2 Tbsp. olive oil, divided
- ½ white onion (40 g), chopped
- 2 cloves garlic, minced
- 1 bunch kale (7 oz./200 g), shredded
- Salt and black pepper, to taste
- 1 cup (150 g) cooked chicken, shredded
- ¾ cup (100 g) parmesan, grated
- 2 Tbsp. lemon juice
- 2 Tbsp. panko crumbs

## STEPS:

1. Preheat an oven to 375F (190C).
2. Heat 1 tablespoon olive oil over medium heat in a brazier/Dutch oven.
3. Add onion and cook for 3 minutes until tender. Add garlic and cook for 1 minute.
4. Add kale and season with salt and pepper.
5. Add pasta, chicken, half of the grated Parmesan, and lemon juice.
6. Mix the remaining Parmesan, panko crumbs, and 1 tablespoon olive oil in a small bowl. Top the pasta with the mixture.
7. Bake uncovered for 30 minutes until the top is golden brown.

## EACH SERVING HAS:

Calories 570, Total Fat 21.4 g, Saturated Fat 8 g, Chol: 175 mg, Sodium 350 mg, Total Carbs: 34 g, Dietary Fiber 1.3 g, Total Sugars 2.2 g, Protein 59 g, Calcium 319 mg, Iron 4 mg, Potassium 636 mg

# PASTA WITH CASHEW SAUCE

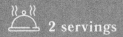 2 servings  10 minutes 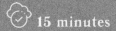 15 minutes

## INGREDIENTS:

- 2 oz. (50 g) fresh arugula
- ½ cup (70 g) peas
- 1½ cups (140 g) broccoli florets
- 1 small white onion (50 g), diced
- 1 Tbsp. extra-virgin olive oil
- salt and black pepper, to taste
- 4 cherry tomatoes/sun-dried tomatoes, halved
- 4 oz. (100 g) whole wheat cannelloni pasta

**Sauce:**
- ½ cup (30 g) fresh basil
- ½ cup (70 g) roasted cashews
- 2 garlic cloves
- 2 Tbsp. lemon juice
- ¼ tsp. sea salt
- ½ cup (120 ml) water

## STEPS:

1. Cook pasta following the package directions. Just before the pasta is done, add in the broccoli florets as it finishes cooking. Take out 1 cup of pasta water, drain, and set aside.

2. Meanwhile, prepare your sauce. Combine all the ingredients in the blender until smooth.

3. Heat the oil in a frying pan on medium heat. Add bell peppers, onion, and seasonings and sauté until tender. Stir in sun-dried tomatoes and arugula and cook for 3 minutes.

4. Toss in the pasta with broccoli. Pour the sauce and add some pasta water for desired consistency. Cook for 4 minutes, stirring occasionally.

5. Garnish with grated hard cheese, if desired.

## EACH SERVING HAS:

Calories: 565, Carbs: 73 g, Chol: 0 mg, Sodium: 55 mg, Protein: 19 g, Fat: 25 g, Fiber: 10 g, Sugar: 15 g

# DESSERTS

# ITALIAN BISCOTTI

# ITALIAN BISCOTTI

 8 biscotti 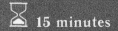 15 minutes 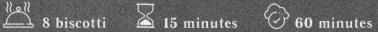 60 minutes

## INGREDIENTS:

- 1½ cups (170 g) almond flour
- 2 Tbsp. all-purpose flour
- 2 large eggs
- ½ cup (70 g) whole almonds, toasted
- ½ cup (60 g) hazelnuts
- 1/3 cup (70 g) sugar
- 2 Tbsp. lemon zest
- 1 tsp. anise seed, ground
- ¼ tsp. salt
- ½ tsp. baking soda

## STEPS:

1. Preheat an oven to 350F (180C) and line a baking sheet with parchment paper.
2. Blend lemon zest, anise, sweetener, and eggs.
3. Add flour, salt, baking soda, and mix until a dough forms. Add almonds and stir to incorporate thoroughly.
4. Spread the dough in a long rectangle on the prepared baking sheet. Bake for 20 minutes until golden brown.
5. Remove it from the oven and let it cool for 30 minutes. Then, cut the dough into long strips at a slight angle.
6. Spread the cut slices in a single layer on the baking sheet and bake for another 15–20 minutes. This will give them an extra crunch.
7. These crunchy cookies are good to dip in tea, coffee, or chocolate milk.

## EACH SERVING HAS:

Calories: 199, Total Fat: 18 g, Chol: 46 mg, Sodium: 99 mg, Total Carbs: 20.9 g, Fiber: 3.3 g, Total Sugars: 10.4 g, Protein: 7.5 g

# BAKED APPLES

# BAKED APPLES

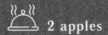 2 apples  5 minutes  20 minutes

## INGREDIENTS:

- 2 apples, cored, but leave a bottom

FOR THE STUFFING:
- 2 Tbsp. honey/brown sugar
- 2 tsp. soften butter
- 2 Tbsp. nuts, crushed
- 2 Tbsp. raisins/dried cranberries/dried apricots
- 2 Tbsp. oats (optional)
- ¼ tsp. cinnamon
- ¼ tsp. cardamom

## STEPS:

1. Preheat an oven to 350F (180C).
2. Mix all the ingredients for the stuffing. Spoon the stuffing into the hole in the apples.
3. Place the apples on a baking pan and bake for 40 - 60 minutes.
4. Serve warmly with a scoop of vanilla ice cream and caramel sauce.

## EACH SERVING HAS:

Calories: 315, Carbs: 62 g, Chol: 9 mg, Sodium: 90 mg, Fat: 9.1 g, Protein: 3.3 g, Fiber: 7.8 g, Total Sugars: 45.9 g, Potassium: 392 mg

# PEAR CRISP

# PEAR CRISP

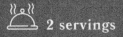 2 servings   5 minutes   10 minutes

## INGREDIENTS:

- 2 tsp. cinnamon
- A pinch of salt
- 2½ Tbsp. coconut oil/ softened butter
- 1 tbsp. liquid honey, plus more for serving
- 1½ Tbsp. coconut, shredded
- 2 pears (360 g), cubed
- ½ cup (40 g) oats
- ¼ cup (40 g) walnuts

## STEPS:

1. Add oats, walnuts, shredded coconut, honey, 1½ tablespoons of coconut oil, 1 tablespoon of water, 1 tablespoon of cinnamon, and a pinch or two of salt to a food processor. Process until it reaches the consistency of a crumble.

2. Heat ½ tablespoon coconut oil in a pan and add your crumble. Cook for 5 minutes, stirring occasionally. Remove from heat.

3. Place the remaining coconut oil, cinnamon, and pears in another pan and sauté for 3–4 minutes over medium heat.

4. Transfer the pear mixture to a serving bowl, cover it with the crumble mixture, and drizzle with honey.

5. Serve with a scoop of vanilla ice cream or whipped cream.

## EACH SERVING HAS:

Calories: 518, Carbs: 58 g, Chol: 0 mg, Sodium: 6 mg, Protein: 8 g, Fat: 31 g, Fiber: 12 g, Sugar: 30 g

# CHOCOLATE MOUSSE

# CHOCOLATE MOUSSE

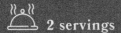 2 servings  5 minutes 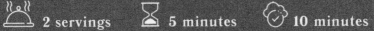 10 minutes

## INGREDIENTS:

- ¾ cup (180 ml) almond milk/ coconut milk/whole milk
- ½ lb. (225 g) dark chocolate, chopped
- 2 avocados (300 g), chopped
- 2 Tbsp. agave syrup/honey/ brown sugar
- 1 tsp. orange zest
- 1 Tbsp. toasted almonds
- ¼ tsp. coarse salt
- ½ tsp. pepper flakes
- 1 tsp. extra-virgin olive oil

## STEPS:

1. Heat milk over medium-high heat in a saucepan until it reaches 175F (80C) on an instant-read thermometer. Remove from heat and stir in the chopped chocolate until it has melted. Set aside to cool.

2. Place avocados, agave syrup, orange zest, and cooled chocolate mixture in a blender. Blend on high until everything is smooth.

3. Serve and sprinkle with toasted almonds, coarse salt, and pepper flakes. Drizzle with olive oil.

## EACH SERVING HAS:

Calories: 725, Carbs: 40 g, Chol: 0 mg, Sodium: 40 mg, Protein: 7 g, Fat: 65 g, Sugar: 4.4 g, Fiber: 16 g

# BERRY DESSERT

# BERRY DESSERT

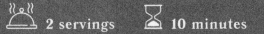 2 servings  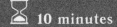 10 minutes

## INGREDIENTS:

- 1 cup (200 g) strawberries/ blueberries/blackberries/ raspberries, frozen/fresh
- 2 Tbsp. sugar
- ¼ tsp. vanilla extract
- ½ cup (120 ml) heavy whipping cream, chilled

## STEPS:

1. Whisk the heavy whipping cream with vanilla extract in a food processor for 2 minutes. Add sugar if desired.
2. Purée the strawberries and sweetener together for the desired texture.
3. Pour the berry puree into serving bowls. Top with whipped cream.
4. Garnish with fresh berries and serve.

## EACH SERVING HAS:

Calories 201, Total Fat 19 g, Saturated Fat 12 g, Chol: 66 mg, Sodium 18 mg, Total Carbs 17 g, Dietary Fiber 1.5 g, Total Sugars 6 g, Protein 1.6 g, Calcium 44 mg, Iron 0 mg, Potassium 159 mg

# DRINKS

# CLASSIC GREEK FRAPPE

# CLASSIC GREEK FRAPPE

 2 servings     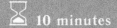 10 minutes

## INGREDIENTS:

- 4 tsp. instant coffee
- 4 tsp. white/light brown sugar
- 4 Tbsp. water
- Ice cubes
- Whole milk/heavy milk (optional)

## STEPS:

1. Combine instant coffee, sugar, and water. Whisk until very foamy.
2. Transfer the coffee to the serving glasses.
3. Add ice cubes and milk.
4. Fill up the glasses with cold water.

## EACH SERVING HAS:

Calories 86, Total Fat 2 g, Saturated Fat 1.2 g, Chol: 9 mg, Sodium 37 mg, Total Carbs 9 g, Dietary Fiber 0 g, Total Sugars 12.8 g, Protein 3 g, Calcium 104 mg

# RED WINE SANGRIA

# RED WINE SANGRIA

 2 servings     10 minutes

## INGREDIENTS:

- 2 cups (480 ml) red wine
- ¼ cup (60 ml) brandy
- ¼ cup (60 ml) orange liqueur
- ½ apple, cubed
- ½ lime, diced
- ½ orange, diced

## STEPS:

1. Mix red wine, liqueur, and brandy.
2. Stir in chopped fruits.
3. Let infuse in the refrigerator for 2-4 hours.
4. Serve with ice cubes, fresh berries or fruits, and mint leaves.

## EACH SERVING HAS:

Calories 389, Total Fat 0.2 g, Saturated Fat 0 g, Chol: 0 mg, Sodium 13 mg, Total Carbs 22 g, Dietary Fiber 2.5 g, Total Sugars 12 g, Protein 0.6 g, Calcium 43 mg

# BLUEBERRY SMOOTHIE

 2 servings     10 minutes

## INGREDIENTS:

- 1 cup (190 g) blueberries, frozen/fresh
- 1 ripe banana, cubed
- 1 cup (240 ml) plain Greek yogurt
- 1 cup (240 ml) whole milk
- ¼ tsp. vanilla extract
- ¼ tsp. ground cinnamon
- Mint leaves, for garnish

## STEPS:

1. Blend together all ingredients in a blender until smooth.
2. Add more milk for the desired consistency.
3. Serve immediately with fresh berries and mint leaves.

## EACH SERVING HAS:

Calories 249, Total Fat 7 g, Saturated Fat 3.2 g, Chol: 22 mg, Sodium 102 mg, Total Carbs 34 g, Dietary Fiber 3.5 g, Total Sugars 24 g, Protein 16 g, Calcium 281 mg

# FROM THE AUTHOR

My name is Linda Gilmore. I am a food journalist and author. I am highly recognized for making culinary magic in my home kitchen. I am also a busy mom of two. This means I am always on the run and looking for any chance to save time and money. I am a foodie through and through at my core, and I have grown into an **advocate for the Mediterranean lifestyle**. With a passion for healthy living and first-hand knowledge of what it takes to stick to a successful lifestyle plan, I will guide you throughout this journey.

The Internet is full of all the information a person might need, but surfing for the right pieces takes a lot of time and effort. Looking for answers to my amateurish questions made me read through countless complex professional texts.

How much did I wish I'd had a book with simple step-by-step explanations? Perhaps, that is the main reason why I've written this one.

*I hope this book will allow you to enjoy the Mediterranean lifestyle with someone special.*

# OUR RECOMMENDATIONS

Mediterranean Meal Prep Cookbook: Heart Healthy Recipe Ideas for Cooking Ahead and Saving Time

Mediterranean Air Fryer Cookbook: Heart-Healthy Mediterranean Recipes for Cooking with Your Air Fryer

# Copyright

Printed in Great Britain
by Amazon

39221170R10066